LIGHTNING ON MY TONGUE

Tina Kendall

ONLYWOMEN PRESS
Radical Feminist Lesbian Publishers

Published in 1994 by Onlywomen Press, Ltd.
71 Great Russell Street
London WC1B 3BN

Some of the poems included here first appeared in *Beautiful Barbarians*: lesbian feminist poetry, ed. Lilian Mohin, Onlywomen Press, London 1986. Tina Kendall has been a writer in residence in Bristol and Bath, Huddersfield and also in Dumfrieshire; since 1992, she's also taught script writing and written and directed films.

Printed and bound in the U.K.

British Library/Cataloguing in Publication Data.
A catalogue record for this book is available from the British Library.

For Annie . . . for the many years

CONTENTS

In Bunches

Checklists

In Bunches

lilies
(for a)

there is an apricot sunrise
in a curled blue sky
a good day feels to be dawning

but there is always the hunger

every two point four seconds
in a faraway country
for want of feeding
a little child dies

i breath in

the last star takes
its cue
and is gone

leaving lemon lilac rinsing
the sky

and the cheerful bustle of birds

this is really the day
when i am free to lay out
mind body and waverings on love
in a cool field under
the sun somewhere

but there is always the hunger

i know i connive am too much
a coward to look myself in the eye
of the mirror of the frothy
meadow-end stream

i breathe in

so many shots in my mind

like the awnings of fields become
bluegreen pools curling
fields where overcropped lilies
rustle and wave in the breeze or stand
still

you can learn a lot about life
from a moment's reflection on lilies
rub your eyes when you notice
every two point four seconds one
of them's gone sucked hard back
into the ground

i breathe in

i must have some tea
take care of myself leave
the low tawny sun for inside

a good day feels to be dawning i
burble time and again till the kettle's
boiled and the lilyfield nightmare is
shrugged away stamped on is gone

the tea scalds my lips
but there are worse things
there is always the two point four second
hunger

columbines
(for m)

there are two winds
i lay my head across your belly

two winds
you giggle in the pink
and purple firelight

flames to tickle your soul

your breasts are firm and tender
do not have to lay a finger
to know

i write wordflames
to tickle your fancy
hearten your soul

there are two winds
your bangles chime and beckon

where am i to go

two winds
i eat my tofu
out of your lap

close my eyes
and see mexican mountains

take me on a camera ride

two winds
and only one of them's
belonging

we know this state outside
eyes close
by heart

pink and purple flames
hiss up with wishes again

while mexican mountains beckon
and glow

so if i lay this sprig
of columbines purple pink
petals of flame

in your lap from me to you

our heads rising way above
the grime of exclusion

two winds blow

shouldn't we just pick up
a writing pad and a camera

and clean knickers

and go?

anemones
(for cmw)

always on the edge

she slides into recognition
automatic smile switch on autumn
sky lips takes without wanting the hair
smell body weight feel of a stranger
lobbing mind to the edge you preserve
thoughts like holy things relics

in her head a sun swept apple orchard trees
aching swarming perfume of waiting fruit
this one the last for tonight then roll
home to the swab plunge scrubbing
the rippling slam thanks of prayer night work's
over and splashing to reclaim the spring
in trampled anemone bath fragrance warmth

the closest she comes to a flower
dead by day

no joy just a snatch at the notes scraping
palms only why can't there be orchards in
cities fresh fruit to replace empty men

wishes unvoiced in the stunned hallow silence
as the water turns chilly for a new thread to
ward off the drowning by numbers a thread to swing
sing begin from

foxgloves
(for v)

pink and blue

foxgloves bow over railway
lines my astral ovary aches

the healer woman tests and then
tells me it all adds up to

unconditional love adds up to

cows smoothing shorn fields
with their bodies day
after day despite rain

and yet i encounter in summer
in cities three swollen women
per minute on average can't

celebrate can't even contact
friends who are pregnant

my astral ovary aches

and the foxgloves swallow
the summer rain bow and drip

unconditional love

passion flowers
(for g)

pure

we sprawl take suck upon
heat bubbled beaches
thick pine grove fencing us
off from the world

dig orange burrows
the sea slash our music by
day until dark

when passionflowers stitch
their hearts up
while we stretch and ignite

shyly cluster of petals

desire sneaks out from
coves chasing the evening glow
to sprinkle our limbs

then you tuck your tongue
inside the folds in my mouth
shaking me on to raise muffled
screams

your flowerhead breasts break up
in my palms and our bodies ply
strings   rains and rains

of scented night music

the passionflower twirls
to the ground

mingling magic and magic and
madness

rose
(for s e)

feed me with light
and dab my sadness with slurring
branches my stove voice turned down
low words no bolder than murmur of sand

feed me   once again with light
i grow more feeble each hour
this war we wage eats all my marrow
my body a rickety frame

the power i disclaim the vision
much too grandiose to be my design
quite alone i would never dare pull
an oasis from desert
build homes and schools and roads
and congregate the broken the unwanted
the dying bring them here to bathe
and rest forever children i alone could
never turn from destruction

nothing is a cause for concern
no despair no panic not a flicker
in the garden of light the power
i disclaim

trouble comes
and dying comes
and loving comes
and chuckling comes

your tingling palms encrusting my neck

come in bunches

and my sisters who can read
lines in hearts and weave their
own square of the cloth
untie suffering for how wide
the day untie suffering when how
deep swig is each dawn

16

sisters who do not smirk
when i say i am drunk with
dance and song

sisters who will come
when dust mingles with
what's left of me
when sleep carries no dreams
of beyond

who will come
to my body adopted
by this land

mutter weak words
since only silence
can check eternity

toss the flower
with thorns   olive
stem and a fragrance
thick as incense offered
to quibbling streams
that they may become
a river

are you keeping track
of how much we're given
and give and the progress
we make along that dwindling
mist path

i have been given dance and song
and have lined an oasis
with the empty and broken
it was easy honestly
fat trees sprang overnight
it all came about quite naturally

the vision much too grandiose
for one alone my sisters slurring
crows on branches lean into each
other curious and eager and still
fighting time

trouble comes
and dying comes
and loving comes

in bunches

and chuckling
i raise both arms
feed me with light
your tingling palms encrusting my neck

then sisters tinge
embalm toss me with
laughter turned heavy
turned light

the one fragile rose

Checklists

checklist

two black sinewy arms check
two framed black legs check
one torso likened to velvet to whose touch check
those unmistakable caribbean ears
the nose and riverbank lips check
and black cum red organs for sex check
flaming lilies on night burnt lakes check
and a hum in the heart call it rhythm of the sun check
trigger of that all-too obvious drum naming stones one
by one in the enclaves of the gods check
and the seeping tones in our voice check
– they speak not of our words – upon which connoisseurs
would not hesitate to slap on the label of black check
and if we move below the skin to where rhythm and voice
combine to steal into sacred musical groves where the lashes
of whips the gashes and stumblings sighs and prayers
are we believe in the final moment of agony sculptured
into something of beauty – all these lanes of suffering and
instruction are flooded with blackness no need for a check
and the food that we feed upon daily crumbling rice studded
with oildripping beans that dissolve on the tongue
and goat curry   spiced back to life and the tip
of mango washed over with lime juice icing throats check
coconut milk to be sucked on and mixed with chilli and nutmeg
and cinnamon cheering up our hungry black noses check
the stories the coming together falling apart black check
and determined still to write black move forward black check
write shake off history's grime spruce up our pride check
but in the end only human we cry dab out our sadness with rum
black check catch hold of anyone clung black check grow dumpy
run off into hiding casting sheets of forgetting over lilies
aflame on night lakes burnt black and hesitate groping for
where our peace place is located having saddled our children
with notions of racism music slavery religion recovery
mandela exploitation the shape of the islands angus bitters
and

culture

untitled

you

walk

and other women watch
you walking

it has something to do
with the grace of your neck
and the swing in your arms
and the lift to your step

it has something to do
with the flight

in your heart

of course
some would say

who is this black woman
that she should raise
her eyes to the sun
and be free

and be proud

who is she that captures
the flickering leaves
and the swaying of flowers
and the shine and the shock

of the waves

she is one not to be shaken by
she is one not to tangle with
she is one to be wary of
she is one to be

watched

ring broken

dropped napkin ring
from my mother's mother's
mother twisted token of kneeling
in dust shattered at night dripping
to candle burn slow ghosts poke
their fleshless fingers feel their
objections rancour settling with the dust

outside the shack time ticks hoarse
gossip rattling the blinds against
gliding caresses of oil
steady steady my mother's mother's
mother's eyes sigh

at dawn you scald swill my threshold
kneading the garden for gold
untouched by their spite their taunts
you shrug laugh and say
old napkin ring who needs cloth
who needs habit i wipe my mouth
on my fingers then your hand
glistens beads of your eyes pin me
in still flashes of blackness
knotting us rope coil caress
through twining oils of the night

laugh while we may scoop
deep as we must of moist treasure
trove tomorrow i'll stride out at noon
brave the glare of the sun
bearing flowers singing to sweeten
the dead

your swimming pool

somehow
as i sweep up
the leaves by
your swimming pool
retribution is shaken
down

somehow
as i sweep into
tiny neat piles
the leaves by
your swimming pool
retribution is shaken
down

somehow
as i sweep into
tiny neat piles
the leaves by
your swimming pool
pick up the clothes
you toss carelessly
to the ground
retribution is shaken
down

somehow
as i sweep into
tiny neat piles
the leaves by
your swimming pool
pick up the clothes
you toss carelessly
to the ground dust
off the chaises-longues
carry into the kitchen
the cocktail debris
retribution is shaken
down

somewhere
as i sweep into
tiny neat piles
the dead leaves of
your swimming pool
pick up the clothes
you toss every day
to the ground
dust off the chaises-longues
you have lounged in for hours
scurry backwards and forth
to the kitchen with
the food and the drink
you have wasted once more
retribution is shaken
and your art deco lamp
by the slip of my trembling
hand to start somewhere
comes crashing
and splintering
down

spring wind
for annie

spring wind i
am in want of
the meadows
          the poppies
cornflowers
          come blow them to
me and in touching
          i'm tethered
          to trying to
          fly you

with me the sky
     slips the earth
turns the wheel burns
     my fingers are burning to(o)
          touching spring flowers

soft token of
trapped in the voice tones
          unheard yet of gentleness
drones the wind blowing
     spring flowers the sun shreds
the light warming down
     and my thoughts fly
my eyes shy
          my lips stick
i'm slipping and licking
     the love that's inside of

  me came on so gentle
          so soft like the spots
of the rain drops the flowers
     bear witness to love in

spring wind

summer break

chalk on mountains
river bed rice boiled dry
and the marble of sunshine

pillowing ribbons of sky
some holiday this

scorching beauty and smothering heat

kick off your sweltering socks
and let deaf stones gobble your feet

chalk on mountains
marking paths we used to climb
spotting ringlets of water

they still sizzled and shimmered last time

parched gaping and sore

like i'm not seeing you any more.

resolution

i'm going to stop saying
i love you because
every time feels like
lopping the top of my finger
off slicing onions

going to stop saying
i love you shut
my eyes to the glory
of autumn trees shake

going to stop saying
i love you stay
home by the fire curtains
pulled shut buried in
books make me look like
i'm busy like i'm learning
and growing

and wait for the winter to come

shadows

sky still heavy with
the shadows of snow

as mystery clicks her fingers

we rub our eyes obeying step
towards the squeak of sun
earth melting under foot

slush touch we

are a valley and a moonrise
are a choir we
sing our hearts soft
as craze of blossom slung into

the newborn stream hearts sewn

into one blaze of belief

mystery steps aside to let
us pass we sing

let noone pluck and scatter we

let noone violate this

Silence in Check
(for mt with love)

(i)

you coughed
we said come on
we said only love
can flatten your heart

you bought a red bike
leather shorts took long
rambling rides and came back
coughing

we said come on
don't think about *him*
snuffing you out
and we made litres of coffee
in your vacuum jug fresh
beans fresh smell and plates
and plates of pasta with mushrooms
– we picked them ourselves – and dollops
of creme fraiche

but nothing
not the bike
nor the food
nor the drink
nor congeniality
– we were always clowning
to get you to laugh –
nor mountainsides mossy
with shiny red sunlight
nothing
could stop you

coughing

(ii)

sydney december '83
what could be more final
than finals?

i knew the score choked
on notes dabbled in bars
whistled crotchets took
to hustling bass
scattering my base

i mean consider the
dramatic possibilities
there were reams of guys
out there newtown was a ripple
i only had to harden my brow
and my eyes pulled up a wriggling hook

till panic came and besieged me
i dived back to my desk after all
what could be more final
than finals?

revision
hard slog through till
midnight then off to a coffee shop
matey slugging cappucino talking foucault
baudrillardderridakristeva you name it
they've read it the sydney illuminati
as pretentious as anywhere else only

more GUTS which is maybe what made me –
my mind lingering on the women and philosophy
as in de beauvoir you name it i've read it
deuxieme sexe wouldn't mind an extra one
myself by GUTS is the stuff it took to – take
the three of them on eyes glinting i swear
my hands were tied or was it my tongue fuck my exams
were finally all over i'd ground my bones working you read me
played squash with a trinity of partners and oh
the belting of the ball my hands were de beauvoir
stitched together so tight i thought i would sneeze

(iii)

after
when i'd stopped
pounding my teeth

we all trooped into the streets
like the mates we'd become
flopped into the coffee shop

(what could be more final than
finals? only three guys hacking you
in two)

drinking espresso cappucino
you name it we raised it foucault
baudrillardkristevaderrida our
household names our holy font

only i can't quite be sure

when we moved on which one of

the four was most Genet

(iv)

it was a stormy night

when i entered the world

felt like it should be
the singing of silence

but the rain raged thunder
battered the tin roofs
till the trees sank

and i was born deep in the night
in a new south wales country
town in the middle of antipodean
winter and my mother confessed

that it pained her a lot

(v)

the lone woman i slept with – knew
it was all wrong all back to front –
died shortly after   believe it
or not i used music any excuse
to swing me away from the island

freeing myself with 'cello and piano
and landed for a time in canberra
town to check out the scene and start to
discover inch by square inch what my real
identity was (had to be something – tap tap
anyone home ? get smart yourself my boy –
beneath that dull exterior . . . i rather
suspected i had a way with wit)

(vi)

you make love i make love
we   make love

i find someone at last to love really love
violins rose petals post-modernism fresh
coffee beans pasta with cream the works

i move in with the guy
who is petit soft as
satin dagger sharp got flung
from a floundering car by his mother
when five thought she was saving his
life only the car didn't crash but he
cracked open his skull an evenement like
that you relive every day which is maybe
what makes him curl into my arms
every night   a september koala aglow

you make love i make love
we make love
in a little tin house
in sydney newtown with cast-
iron curls hanging from the roof
that got left where they were in the war

we make coffee stroke the tension
from our shoulders and necks
and feel as strong and as bright
and as scared as each other

we make love to fight fear

because this is a shred of
the whole this hiccough of
harmony that worries the shit
out of you out of me because
it is too good to happen too good
to exist too BRIGHT

we make love to fight fear
then you hop out of bed
swift as a roo and creep
back upstairs twenty minutes later
sheepish grinning
with coffee

(vii)

you
shiver next to me
with coffee and
biscuits twenty
minutes later i have counted
each second that we sit
up and scoff in the bed
who cares a toss
about crumbs?

a goose-feather duvet
two grown men with lumps
in their throats
three slightly ex-focus
photos of paris sous la pluie
four biscuits to gobble
in inner city sydney
in the middle of a night
when the sea keeps
beating the shore

fighting fear

(viii)

dear phil
i worked out how the sewing-machine
does it sewed together a duvet
cover to hide all the stains very
fetching though i say so myself
and the guy who moved into the house
could be worse but not you glad to hear
you're enjoying the brasseries jazz
clubs i've taken to strolling
along bondi at midnight myself
the witching hour then i yell out
my wanting to the ocean maybe
this hits you splat in the face
as you drag yourself out of bed at midday
and dunk your croissants in that bitter
parisian coffee can't say i'm surprised
you're let down by the french uni system
there was something too ostentatious
too flamboyant about it all not to be fake
the job in the bookshop suits me fine
and i study of an evening – <u>there is a lot
more to old wyndham than meets the eye</u> (my
underlining) or cruise only either i'm aging
or this city's imploding the lumps behind
my ears have been taken back
in by the rest of my generous anatomy
nice of my body really whatever they
were whatever we are they've gone for good
i suppose it only remains to be said that
i miss you (can't write it loud enough)
june is forever away but i'll wait with
a stiff chin or what have you
miss you some more
check you soon

(ix)

let the dead bury the dead
let the dying look to the living
for inspiration

and the living to the dying
for strength to fight on

only sometimes
it's better

not to know
which camp you're in

(x)

chance had delivered his
worst sex-foe into his clutches
change in language from stasis
to machine
from sydney to london
(only one hour by plane to downtown
paris) response to violence
violent repressive grind

form terrible work
and metaphor

i came i had nothing
concrete (italics mine)
to come for but you and
you were in another city
in another land
a handy phone call away

my worst sex-foe was myself
and the wyndham i wrestled with
a shield in my pretended armour
of research but i'd put up with
the lot standing on my head
for the monthly visits when mostly
we would bicker you asserting the
european side of yourself no longer
phil but philippo if you please when
mostly we would bicker
but occasionally
we'd make love
forget fear
until morning

(xi)

i was unprepared for venice
unprepared for further flight
it was a good job anyone could
see that a uni post for up to
seven years go for it man

only london was cold that winter
so much ice in the wind ealing was
the middle of the desert i froze
down to my toenails

we rang and wrote and once
every five to six weeks i'd patter
down on some transeuropean express
that belied its name but you would be
cocooned in the new you the all-
italian you the sweetness and honey

you saying forget france
italy's the true intellectual
centre of europe the *only* place to
be (your emphasis not mine) well
give me cappucino with a dollop of cream

i have got to come clean fuck wyndham
lewis postmodernist theorist it's you
i uprooted myself to be with it's me
that i'm giving on a plate

we eye each other shyly then rush
to the shops where we both buy
the same leather carpet bag
link arms snap a seat in a bar
and you smile at me till the winter starts
to shrivel then nudge my arm point out the
sixteen-year old slouching in the square you
are all froth at some kid who doesn't raise
any glimmers in me i came for your mind we've
stopped making love but that barely matters

this is a cafe in venice a place
i barely belong in and even if our
knees touch and our voices dip
in the same places we've never been so

spittingly far apart

(xii)

i had a mug of fresh
kenyan coffee to hand
when you called to say
giorgio was not a passing
phase giorgio was the start
of a different chapter
un nuevo capitolo
giorgio was where you
wanted to move to

things had flaked out
between us the sex sour as
shit since sydney

we could still be friends

could i by any chance cough
up five hundred dollars till
christmas? some conference
in rome you didn't want to miss

i couldn't gasp
couldn't even force a curse out

you sung in sucked in
check you later
check

(xiii)

lifting myself from
suspended living in
london digging out
a refuge for myself
in de sade country
(apt) close to girlfriends
with a baby and green
cooling mountains that
attracted the sun

the kid tugging my finger
made me feel like i still
had a heart (how do you
kill remembering?) and the
air was so clean it was swollen

maybe that's what triggered
the cough

(xiv)

maybe

it wasn't the cough
that carried him off

and maybe love won't
annihilate an angel

but PMP CMV
chemotherapy radiotherapy
going blind kaposi sarcoma
thrush the constant pain and tests
daily anti-biotics fighting
life and never for a second
being able to forget

all of that would send the sturdiest one
flying

for what could be more off-putting
than this difference derrida?

nothing to write home about
no books to take you in far enough
carry you away

when a grown man can't face
the london (yes back there
again – the flirtation with
france couldn't last long)
streets without make-up to cover
the marks

GUTS is what you need (my
caps) not to mention white
blood cells

what could be more final
than finals

maybe foucault can hasard
a guess or the sailors of
brest go brew yourself
a strong coffee while i
work myself up
to spit it all out (no
danger in spitting only silly sex i
assure you)   right ready?

(xv)

well a third of africa
staggers and drops
and they don't have the cash

to treat all the women
babies and men with the thin
killing disease getting thicker
on the ground

so easy to switch off
the suffering of africa
pretend we are dealing with
a noble whiteman's disease

switch off move on shudder

what could be more final than
a slowly dismembering heart
(the daggers of venice)

what – don't choke on that cough
after all there's still time
to go beyond a surface surfeit
grasp on life
and let it whirl whoosh
all around you

life

what could be . . .

only chicken and leeks
a humble last supper

only not even reaching
the dizzy heights of thirty-three

only hammering the nails
not in your palms in your
coffin

only death

postscript

ocean beach

a deserted swell of
tasmanian strand

like straightened bedding
the perfect place –

he didn't even show for
the funeral –

to toss your soul
this time round

in the shape of ashes

free

games

i do not care to toss heads you
win tails her answer no lie answer
do not care to kick boulders
that line my till now chosen route

turquoise pink creamy sun
rise greets your leaving all
day long feel you going then gone
i find myself sore and aching
from scarlet smile days easing me
to calm places where i want to reside

but cannot so i wonder
when does the eclipse end
sun shift from the moon
too many cogs in the moon
and how do the stars keep
dropping new colours i
get giddy at night spotting

them though my eyes do not own
the same greed the same trust
the same steadiness   now

i know i must not look to you
for oil on troubled conscience
truth carves me up a crazy
ruthless dog i've loved turned
savage and then put down
then lie against smooth
floorboards mourning

i do not care to toss heads you
win tails her waiting to understand
exactly what i need feel want and getting
giddy watching starlight quiver

tsmesis

in the V
        of her arm
a child (she is)
        but

what do we mean by
        modern what do we
mean by contemporary what
        do we mean by

        child

        a schism the wrong
word and the girl shakes
        the child this woman
and loosens her arm
and there is surprise
        concern and no
cushion of wordlessness to
        capture it if
we move forward we forget
what (or subtle tones of
        what) we have left
                behind moved on be
hind contemporary modern
        a girl

over

pantomime rehearsals
making something empty full
i am over

long nights and
polished pubs
over and over

brusque rain drops
at the bus stop
stamping our feet you
flicking the blue scarf
round my shoulders
sending me over

then taking me out home
a christmas surprise
by the candle lamp light
i pushed into your hand remember

remember our mattress a matchstick
sail a beacon we flash
light all over the world
i am over quick

slow slow quick slow slow
quick slow slow slow

then just cling on in wonder
and wail your belly
the centre of my being

your brew full-bodied blackberry
wine i am over

we were laughing on stage
three hours ago here now throw
ourselves into an improvised
second watershow
there are no words but over

perfect enough to sum up
the steam bath we
wallow in together
i am over and over splashing

seals on the coconut cream
water surface no words perfect
enough to describe this stuck
together so deep
except over and over

you are agrin again
tug so tight my breast
i must tip back my
head in delight a moment
can expand to a week
to a year to free from all time
and all i can think is
i'm over i'm over i'm over

when we finally shift ourselves
from this stillness and storm
we notice that even the bathroom
window's covered with coconut snow
flakes nothing is sacred somewhere
beyond this bathroom in which
i am over and over and over

there's nothing to laugh about
but we can blot grief from our joy
can't we no you say somewhere
beyond it's ice cold

the coming and the gone

i nod to what
you give me say
of course say oh
yes that makes sense
is good is what what
what i need baby

nod to the rain spikes
in the wind tambourining
your curved car and then
my body stretching to you
whole body uncurling
anew to the sun that you
bring to me baby

nod to your tombstone and mine
to the not knowing when how with what
to love you but whispering annual knitted
gifts no penance at all for neglect
for this battering blue baby

nod to the rivers that flow
when we talk touch rock rock
rock each other nod to the day
and the night the here now
the coming the gone baby

hospital phone call

i have just had a phone call
from esme who has a garden
full of colours   she tells me

the clematis climbs the fence
and is all purple and the orange
pink gladioli like the flowers
in my room still i can see beyond them

past the african print
what does it stand for
asks colette as if
all needs explaining
as if you can explain
that a line can mean
a memory

that the print is full
of memories of setting
skin on skin

i have just had a phone call
from esme – and i didn't
even ask her what she's wearing
what she's eating how
she's feeling – full of colours

and the nurse removes the phone
and says tomorrow they'll assist
me in a walk outside my room

the afternoon after

my focus shifts

birds are as shrunken
as summer flies

sunday train hurtles by
fields where white horses
swish stamp nuzzle their young

train thrusting me
far far away from
nights of sea spray
beaches scalded into
silence and scattered

footprints of wild golden children
irish whispers
folding me into everything

far far away from other days
of hungry eyes of grey green

so far away

but how do they treat black
people in ireland do rocking
hills aged trees in violet and gold
change a heart

the train hurtles by

and i know yours will do

you see so much

of blue

morning fruit

i had grapes for breakfast
and full juice nectarines
the sun fruit dripped
between my lips
and i was making bright plans
for the future

i had grapes for breakfast
fresh snipped from the vine
and thought of meeting you
at dusk before the shivers come
a bowl of bright plans
for the future

i had grapes for breakfast
and iced smooth melon too
a plane span lace high
in the sky and then my stomach
lurched and i remembered how you
deal in lies to see me and clouds
shut down the sun enclosed
the morning

more

it came suddenly
    what was that woman's name
seemed there would be years more
    the one who died
she was unscarred by disease
    got it now rosemary sloan
kept writing up to the very last day
    we need to get a replacement
soft short sighs over love
    sorted out and such a nice woman
in youth or yearnings for autumn
    well none of us ever . . .
colours not anger at the twists
    i mean death catches you
no breath of husbands beatings
    unawares
she decomposes where lilac
    think about it
sweetens cemetery air
    perhaps we could throw in
a war wrought and ended in the space
    a writing day school
of weeks and the words
    from time to time
and breathless observations linger
    there is such a strong interest
does that not
    these days
give hope
    in creative writing
why should we expect more
    poetry etcetera

expectations

i had thought that in aging
i would become one of those
high-cheeked
elegant
black women
composed
with assurance

. . . . . .

these days
i look in the mirror
often
it's dusty so the image
is deliberately hazy
(it's always the last thing
i clean)
what do i see
a face that's asking
questions and my cheeks
are yet to rise

english

there is a street in
marseilles where all the
sex workers you see are
black women most of them
not even half my age yet

perhaps i even taught
some of them
english

the veil

shadow of war light of life gasping invisible
chalice of battle to soft mouth flesh too weak
to release the words which bring healing peace ecstasy
the screaming of veils rent in two

but who cleans up the warfields
who mops up the pavements of blood

initiates still pay the usual price
for movement for living the rest of us
bludgeoned down further i cannot be sure
flame of spring will score this year
there have been stranger pools of absence
denial

from my lair beyond balance
longings oil me drill me i could say
the faded words i love you
lie there flaunting my body bedecked
in something light tremulous
there is still a wild bird within me
encaged i could murmur love words
wait for ripening pleasure to unfold

but who cleans up the warfields comforts
the dying mops up the pavements of blood
closes the gaping eyes dripping mouths
hardened so many human bodies settled by flies
the survivors more dead than the dead more men
rushing up every day to offer themselves for
the killing

there is still a wild bird within me
encaged bird of prey - will the madness
not even in my darkest sleep in the grimmest
cave of my heart could i free the words
i will kill you and you is as loose
as a cloud in the sky as random as water
dripping - will this madness - must we encounter
the six feet high corpse walls again and again
and again the limbless children - will this madness
not end by invisible hand bringing ecstasy healing
and peace or a veil to strangle once and for all
our humanity with the morning

lightning on my tongue

four spiders slide and weave
    their sticky web
        entangle

        divine toes to spots
like stars on earth
    earth slimy fresh-

       come child chained
    down by every strand
like i to you fingers bracelet

silver hand shine glisten wriggle
       dangling
    above the gaping maze

i speak of stars which shrink
       and then explode i
    dangle in the air across

      your skin half-
breathing as the planets suck me
    in for neptune there's the ocean

of your back
    slow tide you drench and wash me
       wide hoping like the fire

      pent up in mars
to rest a while make sense
    of all that's past

     then burn it burn it free
and hew new caves for loving
      inside we roll

we criss-cross circles
with the sun whispering
words that say this is the starting-

point essential to the whole
as pluto digging transformation
graves

that stop us seeing sense
and words and duty these things wane
but i still lean on you and listen

and observe the spiders spin
their message we perceive
but don't deserve it is simple

it's a journey through light
(will you be waiting there for me
as always tonight?) open my eyes

i read and let the heart beam
strong compassion comfort others
wither wrong   the message

is of crystal (all the colours
of your eyes) so near the gifts shine
glisten explode – or is explosion your touch

upon my thighs? – for all to know
and everybody's raptures sung
i feel too unanchored

too lacking definition to admit
the african spiders' secrets
linking earth earth earth to heaven

or you to me
is

lightning on my tongue